The Game Plan for Success

Learning How to Succeed with Purpose

Garrett Lee

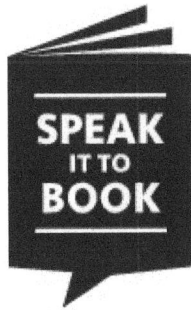

Speak It To Book
www.speakittobook.com

The Game Plan for Success/ Garrett Lee
ISBN-13: 978-1-945793-34-9
ISBN-10: 1-945793-34-1

I'd like to dedicate this book to everyone who has ever had goals, dreams, and aspirations in life and continues to fight their way to the finish line.

You are not alone, my friend.

I hope this book serves as a blueprint that allows you to get to your finish line even faster!

First, I'd like to thank God for allowing me to put this project together. It wouldn't have been possible without Him.

I'd like to give a huge shout-out to my parents—my mom, Rosalyn Lee, and my dad, Gary Lee, Sr.—who have built a strong foundation for me, led by example, and been instrumental to my success thus far. They are a true power couple. They are also the first set of game changers I was exposed to!

I'm very appreciative of the love and support of my two siblings and my sister-in-law—my older brother, Gary Lee, Jr.; my younger brother, Garrison Lee; and my sister-in-law, Naomi Lee. I love all of you!

And thank you to my significant other, Tiffany Taul. Your love, encouragement, and support have helped me in ways you may never imagine. I'm blessed to be on this journey with you!

To all of my friends:
Darrius Norman, Soraya Norman, Mandell Jackson, Stephanie Jackson, Darrell Smith, Jayel Peezodee, Byron Farley, Brian Setzer, Mike Hon, Derrick Williams, Jalissa Hutchins, Rylan Norris, Arianna Dunn, Adrienne Williams, Reggie Casellas, Kristopher Sherman, Briana Medley, John Wright, Allen Ford, Kelsey Harding, David Harding, Tim Averhart, Jacob Spellis, LaDeya Ivy, Nikeya Sharp, Darice Michelle Thompson, Mark Minard, Greg Walker (aka, The Big Dreamer), and Jonathan Boyle—I'm grateful to have such a phenomenal, positive,

and ambitious inner circle of friends whom I can call winners!

To all of my current and previous mentors:
Michael Davis, Greg Walker, David Levy, Felicia Bell, Dr. Jane Sojka, Anthony McCloud, Adison Nelson, Al Riddick, and Jermaine Dixon—all of your inspiring words, insight, and direction have helped me get to this point and progress to higher levels of success!

To my Toastmasters family:
David Levy, Billien McCowan, Emily McCracken, Nicholas Bond, Kyle Burnett, Christina Nadeau, Suzanne Telintelo, Diego Martinez, Bryan Michel, Quiana Barbee, Cheryl Ladd, and Michael Sweeney—you've provided an environment to encourage leadership and growth and have helped sharpen my skills as a speaker!

I deeply appreciate the relationships and personal connections I have with the people who are a part of my life.

CONTENTS

Foreword by Michael Davis

It's June 14, 2014. A young man walks into the room and sits in the front row. I think, "He's awfully young to be here. What is he—twenty? Nice to have a youngster in the room!"

The event is my quarterly presentation skills workshop. Typically, attendees are established professionals and executives working to advance their careers with improved public speaking skills. The young man, Garrett Lee, enthusiastically participates in every aspect of the program. He volunteers to speak, asks questions, and supports others in the room. He is a sponge who can't seem to get enough information.

I think, "This kid is someone to keep an eye on. He's going places."

Fast forward four years. That "kid" has grown to be a dynamic young man who is making his mark on the world.

Garrett Lee has a deep desire to help people live a better version of themselves. This objective is evidenced in his first book, *The Game Plan for Success: Learning How to Succeed with Purpose.* He understands that if you want to succeed, you won't achieve that success simply through desire; you have to *take action.*

But, not just any action. He understands the importance of focused, planned actions toward specific objectives. He offers insights into his journey that has taken him from wide-eyed eager student to highly respected motivational speaker.

This isn't simply a book that you sit down, read, and absorb. Garrett challenges you at the end of each chapter with action steps. In step-by-step fashion, you'll build the foundation for your own success blueprint.

You'll begin with discovering your purpose. This is the 'WHY?' popularized by Simon Sinek in his book *Start with Why.* This purpose serves as the foundation for your goals—a frequently discussed, critical, but often poorly executed aspect of success.

You'll then gain an understanding of how to become better known in your respective field. Whatever your profession—accounting, medicine, entertainment, etc.—you are in business for yourself. In today's competitive and fast-changing world, it's imperative that you develop and promote your brand. This concept—called 'You Inc.' by some—is your best method to let the world know the value you provide.

Finally, you'll receive valuable insight into facing and managing the most difficult part of success—roadblocks, unexpected problems, and the emotional roller coaster every successful person has experienced.

You'll pick up *the* key to managing this challenge: mentorship. No highly successful person has ever accomplished greatness alone. Each one had help—a mentor(s) who pushed when a push was needed and served as a sounding board when venting was required. Garrett provides insight into how to find the best coaches and mentors for you.

Don't let his youth fool you. Garrett is a successful young person because the foundations for his achievements were laid early in life. He has been astute enough to absorb the lessons of the wise people around him. He's studied successful people, sought them out to pick up their knowledge, and most importantly, acted on what he's learned.

This isn't just another success book. It's a roadmap and playbook you can use to jump-start your career or life, written by a young man whom I've watched grow into a leader since 2014.

Do yourself a favor by going through this book and doing the exercises—more than once. When you do, you'll find yourself making huge strides toward the successful life you've dreamed of.

~ Michael Davis, founder of Speaking CPR and author of *THE Book on Storytelling*

INTRODUCTION

Finding Where You Thrive

It's been suggested that most people, even if they aren't buried until they're seventy-five years old, don't truly live after the age of twenty-five.

People reach adulthood and their lives stagnate—they stop truly living. They get stuck in a rut and go through the motions.

See, we're prone to get comfortable puttering through the daily grind. We get boxed in by ordinary living and stop seeking what life could be like outside of our comfort zone. We don't allow ourselves to think about our goals and aspirations.

As a society, we are more exposed to non-authentic reality than to meaningful, realistic information. Entertainment takes a higher priority over personal growth and development. People can tell you about the current reality television shows they're watching, but they don't have a well to draw from when it comes to relevant knowledge.

It doesn't have to be that way.

Exposing yourself to new environments and meeting new people widens your horizon and perspective. It has the power to change your view on life and fill you with the confidence and tools you need to seize opportunities and pursue your dreams.

People can do more than what they think they can. I've seen this play out in my own life and in others'.

For instance, my barber, Allen, devotes time to personal and professional development, and we talk about our goals all the time. One day, he shared his real estate aspirations with me—and something clicked because my mentor had told me about an influential real estate organization in my city. Of course, I passed this information along right away.

So, what could have been an ordinary hair appointment actually turned into an opportunity to further goals.

My Story

About two years ago, working for a company as an assistant manager of an office, I was unhappily caught up in the daily grind. In the back of my mind, I always wanted to do more, but I felt I didn't have the time or energy needed to focus on personal dreams and goals. It was hindering me from reaching my full potential—until a mentor encouraged me to take concrete steps toward success.

And that's the blueprint right there: *concrete steps*.

With society and the business world always changing, you must educate yourself proactively and discover what it takes to achieve your goals. You need to ask yourself: What are the steps involved? What are the possible avenues?

The more you educate yourself, the more you can develop yourself.

Fear of failing will keep you from pursuing your dreams if you let it. For example, I never thought I would be a motivational speaker, speaking to seasoned professionals this early in my career, at the age of twenty-seven.

About a year ago, one of my previous mentors was telling me, "I recommend you target seasoned professionals versus just high schools and colleges."

When faced with that proposition, I was afraid. I told my mentor I was thinking of giving up after receiving rejection after rejection. I told him that event planners were telling me I was too young and needed more experience before tapping into the corporate world.

Companies were looking for more expertise, experience, and credentials than I had. They wanted to see their speakers publishing books and developing solid processes with high success ratings over a long period of time.

Before I had barely tried, I nearly quit. I was giving my mentor excuses before taking the first step toward a new challenge.

My mentor kept telling me I couldn't grow until I got out there and tried to reach new levels. He would ask me, "Are you getting out and networking with professionals, meeting planners, and HR professionals on LinkedIn?"

When I told him I wasn't, he continually reminded me that I needed to put myself out there. Eventually, I took his advice and stepped into those challenges.

It took time, but with persistence, I had my first corporate speaking engagement in January 2017.

Similarly, while working at Enterprise Rent-A-Car, I was eligible for a promotion but didn't proactively pursue it. My district manager called me to the office and went over my goals. He told me, "You need to turn it up a notch. I think you are ready for a new challenge. I want you to apply for a management position."

I told him, "I can't do that. I'm not good in management."

He responded, "How do you know that? Have you been a manager before?"

I hadn't.

He continued, "Well there you go—you don't know you are good at something until you get out there and try."

As I learned from my manager that day, we all have insecurities, but the first step is getting out and overcoming them. If it works out, you have accomplished something to celebrate. But if it doesn't, that's okay too. You try something else. You keep stepping out and taking risks until you find where you thrive.

This book is for people who want to learn and grow. My goal is to motivate, inspire, and help individuals and organizations tap into their full potential through personal and professional development. I believe we all have the ability to tap into our inner greatness, which we might not know exists. We have to get up, go out, and go get! It's all about taking massive action and making it happen.

When we step outside our comfort zone, expose ourselves to new opportunities, overcome our fears, and take risks, there is no limit to what we can do.

As you read, you'll notice I've included a workbook section at the end of each main chapter. The reflection questions and application-oriented action statements in these workbook sections are meant to help you begin figuring out who you are, what success means to you, and how you intend to get there.

Until we try something new, we cannot know what hidden talents we have within our grasp. So don't be afraid of failure, as if failure could ever define you.

Instead, recognize failure as a normal aspect of growing—of developing your identity and life goals.

Trial and error, goals, and mentors are all simply part of achieving success on your terms. Let's start to *thrive* and not just *survive*!

CHAPTER ONE

Building a Strong Foundation

In 2009, a bizarre accident happened in China. One day in late June, a newly constructed apartment building in Shanghai simply collapsed on its side.[1] Fortunately, no one had moved in yet, and the loss of life was kept to a minimum.

Why did this building collapse? It turns out that workers began to dig a parking garage under the building and the entire foundation crumbled.

Without the right support, the thirteen-story building couldn't stand up. In fact, when it fell, it narrowly missed another building close by. A domino effect was avoided by a just a few feet!

Using the metaphor of a strong foundation isn't new to you, I'm sure. Still, it's crucial to start with a strong set of core skills if you're ever going to succeed with purpose.

In this chapter, we're going to discuss several parts of a strong foundation so that you can evaluate yours. If you find that one part or another isn't as strong as you'd like it to be, now is the time to build it up so you can strengthen all the basic areas of your life.

When building a foundation in this day and age, you need four things. First, you need to understand how to build a foundation. Then, once you know what to do, you'll need footings, a foundation wall, and a floor slab.

Key Factors in My Foundation

For instance, the footings, foundation wall, and floor slab that have influenced the foundational development of my character are my parents, my education, and my work ethic, respectively.

Parents/Caring Adults: The Footings

While I was in high school, I worked at Jungle Jim's. One day, my supervisor walked up to me and said, "Garett, you probably have the best parents in the world."

Her comment caught me off guard. I chuckled a little bit, not sure what to say. She turned back, looked me square in the eyes, and said with conviction, "No I'm serious. You probably have the best parents in the world."

I'm sure what she really meant was that she knew, without ever meeting them, that I'd been trained by my parents how to be a good worker. My work ethic, the way I arrived every day on time, and even the way I dressed and groomed myself said a lot about how I'd been raised.

My parents gave me a solid foundation for my life, which is obvious to everyone around me.

That supervisor was right. My parents worked hard to raise me right. I was very blessed to have those two as parents.

My dad was more than just a father to me. He was also my coach when I played soccer and basketball. We did drills together at home to improve my skills. As a team coach, he challenged all of us to work well together and to become stronger.

In addition to coaching me in sports, Dad also was a pastor for a while. From the pulpit, he coached our church to be stronger spiritually.

One of the things that made my dad such a good coach was that he led by example. He didn't just tell me how to be better at basketball: he went out into our driveway and helped me practice.

Similarly, I watched him love people in his congregation when they went through tragedy or needed counseling. Watching Dad helped me to gain a great understanding of what I wanted to be. I learned so many lessons because my father lived them out.

My mom was also there to help keep the structure of our home together—everything from buying groceries and cooking dinner to buying school clothes and keeping a roof over our heads. She worked extremely hard to make sure we had more than enough.

In fact, it's safe to say that my two siblings and I were spoiled at times. Whenever we let it affect our character negatively, she would say, "I hope you understand that you are spoiled and you shouldn't be taking what you have for granted! You have many luxuries and we (Mom and Dad) work hard to ensure you have more than enough!"

I'm proud to say that I never witnessed or experienced my mother going to the club or bar late at night, experimenting with drugs, or sleeping around with other men. My mom has always been a strong, passionate, family-oriented woman. She always did what was necessary to guarantee all of us were taken care of.

However, not everyone gets to have this sort of example. Some children watch their parents run from activity to activity, never having time for their own kids. Other parents show their children the example of drinking, using drugs, or being abusive.

Nobody understands how the example set at home affects us like preschool teachers. They observe children who are three or four years old using adult language or lacking even the most basic manners.

On the other hand, they also see children who have clean clothes and plenty to eat but show signs of neglect or abuse.

A solid foundation in our homes is priceless. It's an advantage we can never buy.

Some of you might be thinking of your parents and feeling just as blessed as I feel. On the other hand, some of you might not have a mom and dad, in the traditional sense, who helped raise you.

Don't feel like you've missed the boat! There are other ways to find "parents" who can help you learn foundational skills.

You don't have to be the biological son or daughter of someone in order to consider that person a parent. A parent can be anyone you trust and look up to—anyone who's a great role model and wants to help can be a parent.

When you find a person like this, who truly has your best interests at heart, you've found a mentor who can parent you in one or many areas of your life.

The critical role that mentors play in our lives cannot be overemphasized. Mentorship gives us the basic understanding that we need in order to function and thrive in the world.

Education: The Concrete Walls

Nelson Mandela once said, "Education is the most powerful weapon which you can use to change the world."[2]

There are so many wise people who have gone before us. When we learn from them, we gain their experiences and perspectives. Why make the same mistakes they made? If we ask questions and study what others have learned, we get to skip so much heartache and many, many errors.

Whether your education comes from a four-year university, a community college, a trade school, or simply lots of good, hard book-study, it will change your perspective.

In addition to learning necessary skills, education also teaches us how to work hard. It's not always the most exciting thing, but this is where we learn to persevere.

I can't encourage you enough to take the time to learn more about your area of business. If you hear of a new topic that piques your interest, learn more about it. Education is never a waste of time.

Work Ethic: The Concrete Slab

Everyone knows That Guy—the one who never cracks a book and still manages to ace every test. Well, I have to be honest here: I have never been That Guy.

All through school I had to put my nose to the grindstone and study very hard in order to keep from failing. There were times when I would watch my friends skate through tests that were hard for me, and I got frustrated.

I'm not the most talented guy, the smartest guy, or the most skilled. But what I am is a hard worker.

As often as I would have liked to be That Guy, I have to admit that I've been grateful for my work ethic even more.

When you're working for success, there are times when things will just fall into place and everything will go right. Of course, these times will probably be few and far between. What's going to pay off for you far more is the willingness to work hard. Whether it's making extra phone calls, working long hours, or studying long after others have quit, hard work will get results every time.

Think for a minute about walking through a parking garage. You probably don't stroll around thinking, "Wow, this place sure has good footings and a solid wall." However, you definitely will notice if the floor you're walking on is cracked and uneven.

In the same way, your work ethic is noticed by others around you. Coaches, supervisors, professors, and clients all notice when you work hard.

Talent is a good thing, but unless it's teamed with a strong work ethic, you'll never reach your fullest potential. There's a saying I've heard that speaks to this: hard work beats talent when talent doesn't work hard.[3]

I've learned that you don't have to be extraordinary to be super-successful. Still, you can be ordinary and do things in an extraordinary way.

Attitude Matters

I have a quote on my desk that I read to myself throughout the day:

The longer I live, the more I realize the impact of attitude on life. Attitude, to me, is more important than facts. It is more important than the past, than education, than money, than circumstances, than failures, than successes, than what other people think or say or do. It is more important than appearance, giftedness, or skill. It will make or break a company ... a church ... a home. The remarkable thing is we have a choice every day regarding the attitude we will embrace for that day. We cannot change the inevitable. The only thing we can do is play on the one string we have, and that is our attitude ... I am convinced that life is 10% what happens to me, and 90% how I react to it. And so it is with you ... we are in charge of our attitudes."[4]

Change Your Mindset, Change Your Path

You've just had a horrible day. You spilled coffee on your last clean shirt this morning. There was a surprise meeting at work and you got reamed out in front of your coworkers. The traffic was terrible on the way home.

The easy path to take is to stomp through the door, yell at your husband or wife for not doing the dishes, bark at your kids when they roughhouse after dinner, and kick the dog when he won't stop growling at the cat.

Once you're on a path of frustration, it's easy to stay there and ride it off into the sunset. What's harder is to take a deep breath and put aside the day's annoyances.

We each have a great deal of power when we feel powerless. I can't control my boss yelling at me. I *can* control my reaction. I can't control bad traffic. I *can* choose to bless the other drivers on the road rather than curse them.

My present doesn't have to be my future. And that's where choosing my mindset comes in. Changing my thought process will make a very real difference to my future. Fixing my attitude now will impact what comes next.

A strong foundation makes this all that much easier. After a bad day, you can call your mentor and ask him to help you get back on track. You can also choose to open your Bible to that favorite verse and refresh your mind. You can throw off your tiredness and put in some extra work to make tomorrow better.

When times get tough, the question becomes:

What are you going to do?

Chapter 1 Questions

Question: A strong foundation consists of caring role models or mentors, a good education (which can include your spiritual background), and a good work ethic. Which of these do you feel is strongest for you? Which is weakest?

_____

_____

_____

_____

_____

_____

_____

_____

_____

_____

_____

Question: Choose one of your weaker areas. Then create a list of two or three things you can do to strengthen that foundational area.

_____

_____

_____

_____

_____

_____

_____

_____

_____

_____

Question: When do you struggle most with having a bad attitude? What can you do to stop and choose a different path next time you're in this situation?

_____

_____

_____

_____

_____

_____

_____

_____

_____

_____

_____

_____

Action: Your foundation will always need to be worked on to keep from crumbling. Write out a list of goals you can reasonably achieve. Revisit the list when you accomplish one of your goals. Feel free to add to it or revise it whenever you feel it's necessary.

Chapter 1 Notes

CHAPTER TWO

Self-Discovery and Your Purpose

Who are you? What drives you? Why should anyone care?

The key to finding your purpose is knowing who you are. We all have unique attributes that set us apart from others. And to truly shine brightly with confidence in this world, you need to know who you are and the niche you can fill.

When you understand *who* you are, it helps you know your capabilities. It fills you with confidence to do things you have never done before. And once you do discover who you are, it's important to be *true* to who you are.

That's something I've been dealing with for the past couple of years. One of my previous mentors made a statement that I took the wrong way—I allowed it to cause me to doubt myself. He was talking about not presenting yourself in a way that brings confusion.

See, I enjoy playing the drums. And when I heard my mentor talk about confusion in presenting yourself, I thought it meant I couldn't be a drummer and a motivational speaker at the same time.

As a result, I stopped playing drums for a while.

But then I remembered a friend who loved coming to my gigs when I was playing in a band. Every time I encountered this friend, he told me I needed to get back to playing the drums because it could enhance my motivational talks. His encouragement reminded me that music is another way to connect with and relate to people.

Just recently at a networking event, a marketing consultant told me that as a speaker, I needed to find out what made me different—what made me stand out.

I thought about that long and hard, and guess where my thoughts kept returning?

To my drums.

And I took them to my next speaking engagement at a high school.

Drumming Up Your Vision Statement

I discovered that I could tie in my drum playing with the message I presented. It was an attention grabber. All the students said the drumming was their favorite part of the presentation!

It was memorable. And as a speaker, that's exactly what you want. You want your listeners to always remember one little detail about your presentation that sparks the meatier parts for them to dwell on.

Playing my drums at the high school assembly was the first time I had done anything like that in such an environment. It made an impression that might stick with them forever.

Through incorporating music into my presentation, I wasn't just entertaining them. I was connecting with them. And that's what many young people are missing: a positive, influential person with whom they can connect.

Through that drumming experience, I learned I could only be myself—and that it was vitally important for me to be me.

The same is true of you. Have you ever stopped doing something that you liked or loved, only because you were worried about what other people would think of you? I thought playing drums wouldn't fit in with motivational speaking because it wasn't "professional." I later learned how the speaking business has changed over the years, and nowadays event planners and audiences are looking for more than just a talking head. They want to be entertained!

This is what helps you connect with your audience. When you connect with your audience, it helps your message resonate with them. This also helps them to take massive action and apply the principles you taught them.

You need to take full advantage of the gifts and talents God has given you. Being true to yourself and using your abilities is what will help you reach your goals. You only know what you're capable of once you do it.

Using all of your abilities strengthens your mission statement. Because at that point, you're not merely talking about your mission statement—you're physically sharing it. You're allowing people to experience your mission statement when you play *your* drums on stage—whatever those drums look like in your life. It opens the door for greater audience connection and gives greater force to your message.

One of my previous mentors would often say, "If you don't know the reason a thing exists, then there's a 90% chance you'll somehow end up abusing it!"

What's *your* purpose? Why do YOU exist?

Companies have mission and vision statements. Those things help define us. It's one thing to know why you exist and what your purpose is, but it's another thing to articulate what your mission statement is. Somebody can say, "I know my purpose," but having a clear and concise mission statement makes such a difference. It adds value to who you are, and it can provide an excellent, professional experience. It helps people know exactly what you are about.

People need to know your specific *why*. They need to know why you do what you do. In business, for example, people get hired because there is something unique and special about them. Simon Sinek, leadership expert, and author of the book *Start with Why*, once said "People don't buy what you do, they buy why you do it."[5]

So what are *your* unique skills and talents that tie into your purpose?

Leaving Your Comfort Zone, Finding Your Purpose!

When I was attending the University of Cincinnati, I did many things that centered on personal and professional development. I did tons of networking within a two-year span. I consider it one of my strengths. And with that skill, I teach others how to network successfully.

My networking ability is an example of something I call soft skills.

Soft skills are unique skills that set you above and beyond your competition while you build your career by making you appealing in your field. If you can hone in on your soft skills and show them to others, they will open doors of opportunity for you.

You and I have a purpose, and it's not to get up, eat breakfast, go to work, come home, go to sleep, and then do the whole thing over again. Life has more to offer—and a significant part of that is discovering your purpose.

So, how do you find your purpose?

First and foremost, it is through experiences such as relationships, careers, business, and family. Our past relationships help guide us to our preferences and what we truly value. They help us understand who we truly are.

Our experiences, failures, and successes help us understand what we are capable of and bring greater clarity to our gifts, talents, and abilities.

For example, I've gotten involved in extracurricular community activities to learn new things and expose myself to new people and experiences. Getting outside of your comfort zone and expanding your sphere helps you learn about opportunities you didn't know existed.

A woman from Procter & Gamble once told me, "Garrett, I think you're a bright young man. I think you're very smart. I think, as a matter of fact, that you're a diamond in the rough.

"However, if you truly want to stand out in prospective employers' eyes, I highly encourage you to get involved on campus in extracurricular activities. Right now, you're just getting off the bus, going to school, going home, and calling it a day. When you graduate, employers want someone who is different—someone who is well-rounded and who can add value to their organizations."

Her encouragement inspired me to get involved in two organizations on campus. One was the UC sales team, and the other was the UC sales leadership club. The UC sales team made a significant impact on my life. It opened my perspective and taught me about networking and other skills that enhanced my professional development.

Those two years on the sales team and in the UC sales leadership club opened me up to many new opportunities and learning experiences. It helped me realize the things that excite me and was a step toward discovering my purpose.

I was forced out of my comfort zone and into the networking experience. I was walking into big Fortune 500 companies, meeting with top executives, and eating lunch with them. I had no choice but to learn networking.

Within the UC sales leadership club, I was the recruiter. I had this role right before I graduated and was scheduling presentations with freshman classes. I would get up in front of a room of thirty or forty people before the class started and give a three-minute pitch on who I was and the organization I was promoting. In no time, I had a lengthy list of students interested in the organization.

I mentioned to my professor how exciting and exhilarating it felt to be in that role. She encouraged me to think about why I was so delighted to be in that role and what about it was so thrilling to me. Doing so helped me understand myself better and showed me that speaking in front of others was a passion of mine.

Those experiences helped shape my mission statement, which is to motivate, inspire, and help individuals tap into their full potential through personal and professional development. My experience at the University of Cincinnati strongly influenced me in discovering my purpose.

How can you start putting yourself in line with more opportunities?

What's Holding You Back from Living, Learning, and Loving?

Some things that can hold us back from discovering our purpose are fear, finances, family, responsibilities, the everyday grind, relationships, marriages, kids, and so on.

I think it's essential not to let anything get in between you and your purpose.

Here's what I mean:

Somebody might say, "Man, I've got to spend time with my wife and family," and use that as an excuse not to take bold steps toward their goals.

In my relationship with my significant other, I know we need to spend time with each other, but we also need to focus on our goals and fulfilling our purpose. I tell her, "Listen, spending time with each other is very important, yet both of us still have things we need to accomplish. So, how about we try to spend more time with each other *while* we're working toward accomplishing our goals?"

We've developed a system in which we sit down with each other and talk about our personal and business goals, including the action steps we will take to accomplish them. This helps us do three things: 1) keep ourselves on the same page; 2) motivate and encourage each other to accomplish our goals; and 3) create a stronger communication connection, which keeps our relationship healthy and strong.

Moreover, we sit down together to work independently. My significant other is a preschool teacher, grad student, and Mary Kay Consultant. I might be sending emails, making follow-up calls, and prospecting for new clients, while she might be creating new weekly lesson plans, working on homework, or devoting time to her Mary Kay business.

What we've learned is that simply being in the same room while getting work done has a positive impact on our relationship and helps us stay stronger longer. Working together in the same room allows for open communication regarding struggles and success stories, and it gives us ready access to a second perspective on how we can be innovative and gain better results.

Fostering relationships is important, and it doesn't have to be at odds with pursuing our goals. Put that excuse aside and make time for both. We must balance our relationships with the pursuit of our goals to achieve our maximum potential.

A bigger factor in being held back is not so much a lack of time or balance, but fear. When we fear something, we avoid doing it because it makes us uncomfortable. If you're afraid of heights, you steer clear of the ladder.

But when you do things outside of your comfort zone, it opens you up to better understand who you are as a person. You discover your hidden potential. It's kind of like opening up whatever doors you have locked inside of your own soul and finding that there was treasure in there all along.

The potential is there; it's just hidden because we've never taken the time to unlock it.

Take risks and see your potential come to fruition!

Living Life with Purpose and the Three L's

In the morning, I take about thirty minutes planning my day and making my to-do list. Those small tasks shape what I do and what I'm all about. They help me clarify my *why*—what my purpose is and how to go about fulfilling it every day of my life.

It's also important to find other people who have similar purposes and engage with them. Two are better than one, so get together with like-minded people and share ideas. Brainstorm ways you can be more proactive in fulfilling your purpose and accomplishing your goals in life.

I like to describe living life using three L's: living, learning, and loving.

Living means taking advantage of everything life offers. Enjoy the luxuries. Make friends. Go on vacation and explore. Live life to its fullest—whatever that looks like for you!

Learning is all about growing from successes and failures, whether your own or other people's. We have to be like a sponge that absorbs lessons from every avenue possible. We must pursue education relevant to our goals and learn intentionally through every life circumstance.

Loving is having love for yourself and others. Love can mean having a child for the first time—it's new, exciting, and life-changing. Love can also be relationships and understanding that all our actions affect ourselves and others and should be motivated by compassion.

The three L's inform your story and bring greater clarity to who you are and what your purpose is. Always remember: you have a unique voice in the world that someone needs to hear. You need not imitate what others are doing, but instead let who you are shine through in whatever you do.

WORKBOOK

Chapter 2 Questions

Question: How would you describe your purpose?

_____

_____

_____

_____

_____

_____

_____

_____

_____

_____

_____

Question: What is your vision statement?

_____

_____

_____

_____

_____

_____

_____

_____

_____

Question: What's holding you back from living, learning, and loving? How exactly will you begin to overcome your obstacles?

_____

_____

_____

_____

_____

_____

_____

_____

_____

_____

_____

Action: Seek and find your purpose. Craft a vision statement to help you stay focused on it, and don't let anything hold you back from pursuing your vision!

Chapter 2 Notes

_____

_____

_____

_____

_____

_____

_____

_____

_____

_____

_____

_____

_____

_____

_____

_____

_____

_____

_____

_____

_____

CHAPTER THREE

Having a Game Plan

If we want to be successful, we must set goals. Trying to be successful without setting measurable goals is like heading to a job interview without knowing the address of the company office. If you don't know where you're going, it's tough to get there.

Goals ensure you have a plan or blueprint that will help you get to the finish line. If you don't have a plan, it will be difficult to get to where you're trying to go. It's almost like you're playing a guessing game and randomly going from one thing to the next with no sense of purpose or direction.

A *Forbes* article I came across, which was based on research from the University of Scranton, claimed that roughly 40 percent of people make New Year's resolutions but only keep them 8 percent of the time.

That's not winning with goals. So, what's the solution?

Keeping goals simple, tangible, and measurable has proven helpful to those who keep their resolutions. So does keeping the goal at the forefront of your attention, such as with a goal board or diary.

In other words, the key to success is "believing you can do it"[6] and keeping it in front of you constantly, like the North Star guiding you home.

Having a Laser Focus

We should set goals for our careers, businesses, and within our relationships, and your goals should focus on taking you to a better place than you've ever been before. For example, how can you get to a better place with your family, your spouse or significant other, or your relationship with God?

In your career-oriented goals, how can you go deeper into your gifts and abilities? How can you get closer to reaching your goals? These questions speak to the purpose of our lives and what we're trying to accomplish.

My goal was to get at least ten speaking engagements this year, regardless of whether they were paid or not. This has led me to be proactive, and each month I focus on doing whatever it takes to reach that goal.

One tool I invested in was a goal planner. A goal planner is a great tool for staying focused and mapping out your goals by writing your most important things to do. They also have sections for people you need to call or text, people you need to email or write, and your plans for the evening. The idea is to keep you focused on your personalized action plan.

Because I am setting simple tasks like this, my focus is getting stronger. I've been spending time invested in my speaking business. For example, on Tuesdays and Thursdays, I focus the entire work day on the speaking business. One of the first things I do is look to see who I need to follow-up with by checking my follow-up list.

After that, I update my social media. Social media is a great networking tool, so I also use it to contact people and seek new opportunities and connections.

I've taken my speaking business to new and higher levels because my focus has been strong. Before this year, I was merely filling up official duties and hoping things would happen for me. However, this year I was clear and focused.

Goals can be personal, too, not just professional. Maybe your personal goal is spending more time with family. Take intentional steps to make that goal a reality. One thing I do to make that happen is take my immediate family out to dinner periodically to catch up, so they know how much they're appreciated.

As you set daily goals, track your progress. Are your goals measurable? Can you easily discern whether or not you're moving toward accomplishing them each day?

I have a goal board. Each month I put my goals on either the short-term or long-term goal board. Goals that have a three-year time frame go on the long-term board, and monthly goals go on the short-term board. This helps me keep in view what I'm trying to achieve over time and gives me a tangible way to measure when I have fulfilled my goals.

Intentional Challenges

When you set goals, you need to challenge yourself so you will be truly committed. Set challenging goals, write them down, and commit to seeing them through.

If you don't challenge yourself, you will be less likely to make it to your finish line. You will live an average life stuck in the daily grind. Don't merely talk about your goals while doing nothing to reach them. If you take the initiative, you're already on the right track. I have a program on which I present titled "Get Up! Go Out! Go Get It!" which is all about taking initiative and realizing something different needs to be done to start creating the results you are looking for. When you simply "show up," you're already halfway to the finish line.

Setting challenging goals will enable you to know where you are going and encourage you to invest the commitment necessary to get there.

It also helps to have like-minded people around you to hold you accountable. Build relationships with people with whom you can talk about your goals. Find a support system that will encourage you to take real steps toward your goals.

Setting goals is about taking one step at a time. The fact that you have a goal already puts you one step ahead of many other people. Now it is important to go through the process and do the work necessary to go the rest of the way so that you experience massive success!

Don't get weighed down worrying about how you'll get there. The important part is to take one simple step *today* toward your goal. If you do that enough times, guess where you end up? At your goal—and without all of the worry. "As long as you make progress," one of my professors once said, "you are successful."

Everything we do in life should be intentional. We shouldn't wander from one random thing to the next. This is what makes goals so valuable.

Setting goals gives us direction and purpose. It helps us stay disciplined as we choose the path in life we want most—instead of never honestly trying because reaching goals sounds too difficult.

Which path sounds more attractive to you? Which do you think will make you happier over the course of your life? Which will leave you satisfied at the end of your life, reflecting back on your journey?

Think on that, then start writing down your short-term and long-term goals.

WORKBOOK

Chapter 3 Questions

Question: What planning tools do you (or could you) use to help maintain your focus?

_____

_____

_____

_____

_____

_____

_____

_____

_____

_____

Question: In what other tools or resources could you invest to help you "go deeper" in pursuit of your vision?

_____

_____

_____

_____

_____

_____

_____

_____

_____

_____

_____

Question: What are some specific, intentional challenges you could pursue to further your vision?

_____

_____

_____

_____

_____

_____

_____

_____

_____

_____

_____

Action: As you pursue your vision and goals for success, create a plan to hold yourself accountable. Invest in specific tools for success, but also seek out challenges that will advance your vision.

Chapter 3 Notes

CHAPTER FOUR

Yes, You Have a Personal Brand

Imagine you are taking a walk outside and you notice someone giving away free iced coffees. As you approach the table, the person says you have a choice: you can have a Starbucks iced coffee or a generic iced coffee. Which would you choose? Most of us would probably select the Starbucks iced coffee because of how well known the Starbucks brand is.

Your personal branding is equally important, so people know what they are getting if they hire you.

When I go to high schools and colleges, I ask the students what comes to mind when they hear the term "personal brand" and what that means to them. Usually, the response is a list of products or big companies like Nike.

I explain that our personal brand is how people perceive us. The way you walk, talk, carry yourself, and interact with people on a day-to-day basis affects your personal brand.

Whether you realize it or not, you carry your own personal brand. So why not use this to your advantage?

From the Elevator to the Pond

Personal branding starts with a mission statement. People must understand who you are and what your purpose is.

Visualize yourself on an elevator for over thirty seconds. While on the elevator, you come across the decision maker of your dream job. What do you say before you have to get off the elevator? What speech do you give?

The elevator speech should answer three questions: who you are, what you do or want to do, and why anyone should care.

Regardless of where you go in life, you will always be selling yourself—and you have to know what to say. You need to know how to communicate your personal brand and why it exists.

Your image is another significant component of your personal brand. Your image is the way you dress, your hairstyle, and what people see when they look at you.

A final component is communication—both verbal and written, such as the way you communicate online. Your ability to communicate clearly will show your level of professionalism.

Your actions have to line up with what you present as your personal brand and who you say you are. You can talk the talk—anyone can do that—but are you walking it out? Does your life back up how you've presented yourself?

For growing your brand, you need to be consistent and have clarity on what you stand for and want to convey to others. Who are you hanging out with? Who are you learning from? What is influencing you? Who you spend your time with will either enhance or hinder your personal brand.

Staying true to who you are is crucial. Don't exaggerate and oversell yourself in a way that isn't an honest representation of who you are. Instead, keep your personal brand 100 percent real. That's staying true to yourself and the absolute best way to market yourself.

Owning Your Personal Brand

Communicating your personal brand through your authentic life puts you in a position to become successful. A perfect example is how you present yourself on social media.

When I talk to students, I tell them this is the digital age, so we love our technology. Nowadays, networking is about social media. Everyone is on various social networking platforms such as Facebook, Instagram, Twitter, and Snapchat. The way we communicate on those platforms tells a story about who we are.

For instance, I'm a life skills coach and motivational speaker. Now, if I get on either my personal or business Facebook page and post crazy pictures of the weekend getting hammered, or of me with half-naked women, people will perceive I am not professional and not who I say I am. When people look at those posts, their perception will differ completely from what I want my personal brand to be. It will diminish their view of me and hinder my professional platform.

When a person or company is considering me to speak to their audience, they will definitely research who I am. They will most likely search for me on Google and visit my social media pages. Their view of my value will largely come from what they see when they visit my social networking platforms. The way I present my personal brand on social media will affect their decision.

When I'm communicating with event planners, they typically don't know who I am from the get-go. Many want resources so they can see who I am and what I am offering. They want to see me in action through live video footage. They expect me to have marketing materials that showcase my personal brand.

Often, I send them links to my website, some video testimonials, and a promotional video I had made. Ever since then, I've noticed a positive correlation with more speaking engagements. Doing the work to develop your personal brand will only further your career and open more opportunities for you.

There is a big event called the Small Business Festival that has taken place for a couple of years now. Microsoft helped power the festival, so at different Microsoft stores throughout the country, they held Small Business Festival events at which people came out to speak on different topics.

Prior to the most recent Small Business Festival, I applied to various local festival events to speak at Microsoft stores from St. Louis to Chicago to Atlanta. At the last minute, I got a phone call from Microsoft's community engagement director.

She reached out and said, "Garrett we've noticed you've been applying for various speaking opportunities at these stores. There's a last-minute opportunity that came up in St. Louis. It's a lot closer to home than some other opportunities you've been applying for." She specifically said, "I saw your promotional video, and that's exactly what we're looking for."

I knew that was the only thing she saw of me because I have limited footage, information, and video of me online—for a reason. I have it set up so when people see my personal brand online; it matches what I want them to perceive of me professionally.

I have plenty of video testimonials, but I don't have a single video of an entire speaking engagement I've done. An event planner doesn't have the time to listen to somebody's full presentation. I also don't want to diminish my value as a speaker by allowing my entire product to be available for free online.

If I post anything online, it will be a short testimonial video, a quick promo video, or two to three minutes of my presentations to serve as a teaser for interested individuals as well as event planners who are looking to bring me on board to speak at their events. This targeted personal branding is exactly what landed me the speaking engagement for the Small Business Festival.

Based on my promo video, she saw I was what they were looking for. They valued what they saw and agreed I was the person who could help make their event impactful and memorable. They wanted me to come in and help represent Microsoft and the Small Business Festival. That showed their perception of my personal brand was valuable.

It's important for you to understand you have a personal brand that impacts your day-to-day life. Everything you do is communicating to others who you are—and it will ultimately affect your future in a big way.

It's All About Promotion

You must put yourself out there and represent your personal brand. I went to school for marketing, and there are 4 P's of marketing. Two of the four are place and promotion. These are strategies businesses use when branding a product.

Place is all about being present and visible so people can know who you are. You need an online presence so people can easily discover you. Having a website or other online platform makes you more visible.

Every business needs a website. A website increases your level of value, allows you to control your personal brand, and makes your business easily accessible to your clients (or potential clients).

Having a website could be what sets you apart from your competition. If an event planner is deciding on bringing in one of two speakers, and one person has a website while the other doesn't, the event planner will likely choose the speaker with a website. You greatly increase your professional reputation by having a quality website.

Even for the regular professional, a strong, positive, and professional online presence is invaluable. For example, a recruiter or an HR representative turns to LinkedIn to find potential employees. Having a LinkedIn account alone can increase your chances of exposure. Recruiters and HR representatives want to see your personal brand represented professionally on LinkedIn.

We need to communicate our personal brand in ways other people can relate to. For example, on both my personal and professional Facebook pages, everything is pertinent to what I do. I'm always reminding people I'm a motivational speaker. But I also keep it relatable.

You won't see me in suits on everything I post on Facebook. I post things about working out. On my last workout post, I said, "Despite it being Sunday and Memorial Day weekend, I'm at the gym getting my mind right and keeping my body in shape so that I can live a healthy and fulfilled lifestyle." I talked about how there's no such thing as excuses, only opportunities, and then I transitioned and said, "The last time I checked, you can't deposit excuses at the bank."

Even when I post on Facebook about working out and health, I always tie it into a message that uplifts and challenges others. Yet I do it in a way with which everyone can identify.

Promotion means you must promote your brand—in an honest way—via paper, person, Internet, media, or word of mouth. In fact, word of mouth is the easiest form of promotion. Some of the best business links are referral-based. So get yourself out there! Promote your brand through any and every available means.

Your online presence, the way you carry yourself, how you dress, and how you communicate all dictate how others perceive your personal brand.

Your personal brand not only helps you appreciate yourself but also enables you to stand out from others in the eyes of prospective employers and clients. Remember the Starbucks example! When a potential employer is trying to decide between hiring you or hiring someone else who is equally qualified, your personal brand will be the deciding factor.

Ultimately, it's important to have a winning personal brand so people can have a clear vision of you—so they understand who you are, what your purpose is, the level of value you want to attract, and the direction you're heading in.

WORKBOOK

Chapter 4 Questions

Question: If you had only the time of an elevator ride to convey your personal brand to a potential client or customer, what would you present as your mission statement?

_____

_____

_____

_____

_____

_____

_____

_____

_____

_____

_____

Question: What are the specific aspects of your brand? What do they communicate to potential clients or customers?

_____

_____

_____

_____

_____

_____

_____

_____

_____

_____

Question: How do you (or could you) promote your personal brand in social media? How could you better promote your brand in face-to-face situations?

_____

_____

_____

_____

_____

_____

_____

_____

_____

_____

_____

_____

Action: Own your personal brand by having a mission statement. Be deliberate but honest as you put yourself out there and proactively shape others' perceptions of you— in social media, in person, and any way you can!

Chapter 4 Notes

CHAPTER FIVE

Networking—A Matter of Relationship

In the '90s, three college students invented the parlor game Six Degrees of Kevin Bacon. These young men realized Bacon was well connected in Hollywood and could be linked to almost anyone in the industry in a chain of six or fewer people.

These sorts of extended connections are what networking is all about. We never know which relationships will lead to that next job, but getting your name out there matters. Almost every opportunity I've had has resulted from networking.

Networking is more than simply handing out a business card. It is making connections and building relationships. If you go to a career fair or networking event and come across somebody with whom you have a connection, that is the person to whom you want to give your information.

If you talk to somebody and the relationship looks like a good fit, or you feel you might do business with or learn from them, hand out a business card—and later, follow up with that person.

This is how new opportunities begin: you make the connection and follow up. From there, you may receive a phone call or perhaps an in-person meeting. And if these go well, opportunities tend to follow.

Who Are These People?

Meetings, phone calls, and emails are all part of the rapport-building process in your relationships and connections as you network. Even if those encounters aren't directly related to business, it is valuable because that's how you build trust as you deepen the relationship.

Through these interactions, the people with whom you connect will trust what you do and who you are as a person. Not only will that make them more likely to do business with you, but they will also have the confidence to recommend you to others.

When you make these connections through networking, you have to take the initiative. You have to remember that *you* are interested in fostering the connection. *You* handed out the business card. So *you* need to be the one to pick up the phone and follow up.

It's all about keeping in touch and building the relationship. If there's an opportunity to go out for happy hour, coffee, lunch, or dinner, take advantage of it—because those things show you're truly interested in getting to know the person both personally and professionally.

Building relationships is all about building rapport with somebody. You trust each other with mutual disclosure and open up to learn more about each other. Through this process, you discover each other's strengths and weaknesses. You learn about potential opportunities that extend beyond your relationship.

Never underestimate the significance of an opportunity set before you. It takes time to explore the opportunities present with each connection you make. As the saying goes, "Don't judge a book by its cover." Dive into the content first to see what's what.

Seek to make genuine connections without having an agenda of gaining from it professionally. Don't hold your hand out as if you're looking to get something from somebody. If you are seeking what you can get out of people, you will miss out on building a sincere, mutually beneficial connection.

When you follow up, always let the person know that you are engaged with them and available to benefit them. Let your actions show that you're interested in creating a relationship advantageous to both parties. Before you even ask for any help or a business referral, make it clear you're willing to help them in whatever way you can.

Whenever we want something big in return, we need to prove we can be trusted with the small things. As the Bible says, "One who is faithful in a very little is also faithful in much…" (Luke 16:10).[7]

What I've learned in building and maintaining relationships is that the little things matter. Making small connections is essential for keeping those connections going.

Investing in networking connections doesn't have to be extremely time-consuming or taxing. For example, when I have a speaking engagement, I reach out within twenty-four hours with a friendly thank you. I may even write a thank you card or offer another small gesture of gratitude.

Your message can be as simple as saying, "Hey, thanks for the opportunity! I had a great time speaking at your company and engaging with your employees. I thought it was a great outcome. Let's definitely keep in touch for future engagements."

In building genuine connections and relationships, it's important to keep asking yourself, "How am I coming across to this person? How am I communicating with this person?"

Not Your Average Weight Lifter

Networking certainly doesn't have to be an awkward, formal experience. When I go to companies and schools, I find that people tend to think networking is more complicated than it really is. They are nervous and scared because they think it's a formal experience.

People freak out, saying, "I'm not sure how I will come across to people. What if it's a very important person? What do I say? What will they think of me?" But networking doesn't have to be intimidating.

Networking takes place everywhere. It's not just going to a career or networking event—people network at bars, restaurants, business events, grocery stores, and even at the gym! I have networked in all types of places.

I lifted weights at the gym with a guy named Derrick. One day I asked him, "Hey Derrick, what do you do for a living? We are always talking about physical training and sports, and you seem like a cool guy, so I'm curious what you do."

He responded, "I work in sales for a company called Enterprise." It made me curious because I was in college and interested in learning about sales opportunities. So he said, "You can call me whenever you want if you have questions. I have a bit of other experience in sales, and I love this company." That relationship helped lead me into an opportunity with Enterprise.

Here is another example from the gym. Once I noticed a guy lifting whom I had never seen or talked to before. We came across each other while working out and engaged in small talk, and I learned his name was Bruce.

He asked, "Are you in college? What are you doing right now?"

I said, "I go to the University of Cincinnati, and I'm a business student looking for a sales position. I'm actually in the interview process for Enterprise."

Then he said, "I know one of the top guys who works for Enterprise. Let me know and I will put you on the phone with him."

I didn't follow-up with him. But when I saw him at the gym a week later, he said, "Hey what's going on? You never called me. Listen, I can take you to the well, but I can't force you to drink the water. But you know what? I'm putting you on the phone with this guy right now."

He stopped what he was doing and called someone named Kwesi. He said, "Kwesi, I want to put you on the phone with this guy, Garrett. He's interested in the sales position as a management trainee at Enterprise Company. Here's Garrett for you."

He handed the phone over, and I talked with Kwesi. He seemed like a nice guy and tried to sell me an opportunity with Enterprise even though he wasn't a recruiter. We talked no more than five minutes, and I was thankful for the opportunity.

I called him a few days later because I had some questions after my second interview with the company, so I said, "Hey, I want to follow up with you. I got done with interview number two. Thank you for taking the time to speak with me the other day and for all the insight and wisdom you shared with me."

He said, "No problem! I'm sure you will get this job." He said it like it was no big deal.

I responded, "Really, why would you say that?" He said, "Everyone in HR likes you a lot, man. I'm sure you will do just fine."

During the last interview, I told the Enterprise interviewer about all the people I knew in Enterprise, and I mentioned Kwesi. He said, "You know Kwesi? His office is just down the hall. I'll take you to his office before you leave."

He took me to Kwesi's office, and we all talked about sports. A couple of days later, I got a phone call for a verbal offer for the position. That entire experience led back to a connection that came from a simple talk at the gym.

Networking is developing sustainable relationships. When all is said and done, success is based on two things: what you know and to whom you're connected. If you take the time and effort to connect with others genuinely—even in small ways—you will be amazed by the opportunities that open for you.

Go to conferences and networking events. Pursue opportunities to expose yourself to situations that will further your life pursuits. One of the top two reasons people don't achieve their dreams is because of lack of exposure.

Just as Kevin Bacon can be connected to anyone in the Hollywood business with six people or fewer, we want our name to be in as many network pools as possible so we can easily be found.

It takes time to network well, but the effort pays off.

WORKBOOK

Chapter 5 Questions

Question: How can you broaden your network? What is one promising potential connection you could pursue?

_____

_____

_____

_____

_____

_____

_____

_____

_____

_____

_____

Question: How, specifically, will you initiate a relationship with this potential connection?

_____

_____

_____

_____

_____

_____

_____

_____

_____

_____

Question: How exactly do you follow through after initiating connections?

_____

_____

_____

_____

_____

_____

_____

_____

_____

_____

_____

Action: When you engage in networking, focus on forming genuine relationships. Build real rapport with people as you work to create a connection. Then follow up with them, simply but sincerely, after you establish an initial connection.

Chapter 5 Notes

CHAPTER SIX

Mentors Can Be Game Changers

Sometimes, there's nothing wrong with taking shortcuts. Mentors are the perfect example.

One of my current mentors is Dr. Jane Sojka, who was my marketing professor at the University of Cincinnati and taught the class Professional Selling. At first she didn't know me, but she was bold—because she cared about me—and told me, "Garrett, I'm curious about you."

Dr. Sojka continued, "I want to learn more about who you are and your future. Let's meet in my office."

For about thirty-five to forty minutes, she got to know me. From that day forward, she would boldly tell me things I didn't want to hear or things she thought I should do—for instance, "Listen, I think you need to cut your braids off." And she would tell me why it was important: "I've got you in front of these executives, and I want you to be as polished as possible. Once you become that CEO, you can grow your hair out and do what you want, but right now I want you as well-groomed as you can be."

She would tell me straight up how she felt and explain, "I don't mean to offend you. I want to get you where you want to be and give you access tips to make sure you get there."

Though they may sometimes say things you don't want to hear, mentors can be game changers in your life. They can see years ahead of you, help you learn from mistakes and successes, and ultimately push you to reach your goals sooner and more effectively.

What Makes a Mentor?

Mentors, in short, allow you to shorten your learning curve. They can shave years off of the learning process, which results in you going further, *faster*.

Mentors bring their experience and allow you to learn things you didn't know. They educate you and open your perspective. They can see right through you and often grasp things you never knew existed before they pointed them out.

And they have that special ability to bring you to a place where your light can shine.

A mentor is someone who already lives where you want to be. They've been through the journey and can share hardships and struggles from which you can learn and grow—instead of you needing to endure those same hardships and struggles.

Learning what not to do and focusing on what to do instead represents a shortcut. This is what mentors make possible.

It's Not About the Camera

I'm a part of an international organization called Toast-masters, which centers on bringing in guest speakers to hone and develop members' public speaking skills. I went to one of my first meetings about three years ago, and this is what happened.

I Googled "professional speaking coach" and a guy named Mike Davis came up. He was scheduled to be a guest speaker at a local Toastmasters club, so I showed up (late, unfortunately) and connected with Michael Davis face to face.

When I met Michael, I introduced myself and told him how I had found him on the Internet and heard he would be the guest speaker. I explained I knew he was a professional speaking coach, but I had missed hearing his message. I gave him a brief background about who I was, and he was very impressed.

He immediately gave me his business card, told me about what he does, and invited me to schedule time to meet with him because he would love to shave some years off for me. I met with him and found out he had a workshop about a month or two later, which I attended and where I learned some great material and connected with like-minded people.

I could call Michael if I had questions and he wouldn't mind—no scheduling or paid consultation necessary. He allowed me simply to reach out, and he would then give me feedback on my website or go over a presentation I was putting together. He was a down-to-earth person who happened to live in my community and who humbly helped me out.

Later, I joined a local Toastmasters club, and around my second or third meeting, I volunteered to be a guest speaker.

When I showed up, the first person I saw was Michael Davis.

"Man, I didn't know you would be here," I said.

He was also on the schedule to be a guest speaker. We both gave speeches that, ironically, happened to be centered on the same message—the power of purpose.

After the presentation, Michael gave me specific advice that went deeper than the normal feedback given at these events. He said he thought I'd done a good job overall, and then he went over opportunities to improve.

Michael said, "I noticed you focus much of your energy on the camera. Try not to do that so much in the future. If you're focusing on the camera, it seems almost like a television recording, and if it's a paid opportunity, then something like that can cost you."

He continued: "Some people will cut you for that, and I'm telling you because of our relationship. I understand where you're looking to go and you're not just a beginner."

I had no idea it was a big deal; it was something I didn't know I was doing.

From that day forward, I changed my speaking style— and instead of losing money, I've gained it.

Calling It Like It Is

Another experience occurred after that same event, where I met another one of my mentors, John, who was the club president. Later on, he became my coach.

When I met with John, I learned quickly about his strength and talents. He was an amazing speaker, a phenomenal leader, and a great entrepreneur. This guy could truly understand where I wanted to go, and he understood the potential obstacles at an early stage.

In my mind, I already knew he would be my mentor, and I assigned him this role not long after I met him. Whenever I saw him, he would ask questions to see where I was at. If I wasn't making progress, he would call me out.

Mentors earn the right to do these things. They call you out and provide positive, constructive criticism for your personal growth.

And John would always challenge me about giving him the same excuses. He would say, "Listen, you have the right people around you—there is no excuse."

We had one specific conversation about a year ago when I was feeling frustrated and down in spirits about where I was in my speaking business. I even told John I wanted to give it up and would try a different direction.

He said, "First, I never told you things would be easy. Any entrepreneurship venture is not easy. If it were, then everybody would do it."

Then he said, "When you get frustrated, that's not the time to throw in the towel. That's the time to sit back and reevaluate your situation."

When you get frustrated, and things aren't going your way, evaluation could reveal several things. Maybe it's the way you're approaching the venture, your attitude, or specific actions you're doing or not doing.

John said, "Listen, you have special gifts and talents that God has designed you with. He's given you these for a specific purpose, so it's important to know that and to capitalize on it."

I tried to offer excuses about me being young and not having experience. I tried comparing myself to people like Tony Robbins, and John said, "How can you compare yourself to somebody who has decades of experience in entrepreneurship and life coaching? Everybody had to start somewhere, and you can't compare yourself to people who have years of experience when you're just starting out. That's an insult to yourself."

John continued, "It's not all about the credentials. It's about you capitalizing on your strengths, talents, and gifts—then going after it and staying positive."

He also observed, "I see you're spending all your time and energy reaching out to these high schools and principals. Garrett, I keep telling you, you can give these same messages to the corporate arena."

Then he asked me, "Are you capitalizing on your social media? Are you connecting with small business owners? Or are you connecting with human resource representatives of different companies on LinkedIn?"

I think it was the experience of this specific talk that helped change my mindset and pushed me toward my ultimate vision of success.

But even today, whenever I talk with a mentor or coach, I find it's so uplifting to have somebody who can see through you and to envision what you're capable of. It empowers you to push through and get to that finish line.

Mentoring Versus Coaching

Once, John explained to me, "There is a difference between mentorship and coaching. The mentor will tell you what needs to be done to get to the finish line. A coach is someone constantly riding you and touching base with you, someone who is more actively involved and even makes you feel bad when you need to."

My mentor relationship with John is one where I could call him asking for advice and he would guide me in the right direction.

Since John does coaching programs, I asked, "You know, with me, what you think? Do you think I would benefit more from the mentorship we already have going on, or from a coaching opportunity with you?"

And he said, "You have mentors, but you have to be careful. You only need one at a time. I think you need more coaching. You need somebody who sits down with you and does more and takes you deeper." So we agreed to follow up with another call about a possible coaching opportunity with him.

Coaching is more focused than just touching base. It's more of an investment to go further and at a faster rate.

How to Find a Mentor or Coach

A mentor must be highly qualified and someone you can connect with. You need a mentor who is trustworthy, open, and approachable—not to mention, someone who has reached a point in life you eventually want to get to.

If I come across somebody genuine who wants to give back and can show me their struggles, their successes, where they are, and how they got there, then they've got my attention.

The first step when you find a like-minded person is to connect. It's simple, really. Start with some small talk. Afterward, if it seems right, ask if you can stay in touch with the person and maybe get their email address or phone number.

Then follow up with purpose. Let them know you enjoyed meeting and connecting with them, and tell them that you'd benefit greatly from learning from them.

Like networking, mentorship does not have to be the awkward, formal experience we sometimes are led to believe it is.

Mentoring in the Rain

A mentor is a role model to whom you can look up and reach out for advice—someone you can learn from, who enables you to grow as a result of being around them.

That doesn't mean it has to be in a professional setting or always at a scheduled time. Mentorship can take place during a fifteen-minute talk.

In my full-time job, I work as a sales consultant or a product specialist at a dealership. Early in the afternoon, my sales manager approached me at the beginning of the shift and told me a customer was outside in the rain. So I got my umbrella, and by the time I got back up front to head out the door, there was another salesperson already going to the customer. My sales manager noticed how I didn't have a high sense of urgency to go outside to help the customer immediately.

My boss came back over to me and asked, "Hey, Garrett, do you have a few minutes to talk?"

I said, "Yeah."

So we talked in the conference room. "How are things going?" he inquired.

I replied, "Not the best." He asked why, so I explained, "Well, I think it's a combination of having bad luck this month and maybe needing to change things."

Then he said, "I want to stop you right there. I don't believe in bad luck. I don't believe in *luck*."

I knew his mother had suffered a stroke and was living off a feeding tube at the time. "Now, let me tell you what you don't know," he said. "We give my mother and father money to pay into their healthcare plan. But without telling us, they stopped paying into it."

He said, "My mom and dad won't go to the doctor or get help unless they don't have a choice. If you tell them something, they just won't do it. We found out recently my mom was having a series of seizures we were not aware of."

He continued, "Do you think my mother's current situation is bad luck, or what do you call that?"

And I said, "I call that an unfortunate situation."

He said, "Yeah, it is a bad experience and unfortunate situation, but it has nothing to do with luck. Our today has directly resulted from everything we did yesterday, and everything we put in today will affect our tomorrow."

Through conversations like this, mentors can become game changers. They can see years ahead of you, and they are in a position to help you learn from their mistakes and successes so you can cross the finish line faster.

Find mentors in your life who will invest in you, speak truth to you, and walk alongside you. Select your mentors carefully—they should be people you admire and want to emulate in some aspect of their life.

Mentors provide invaluable wisdom and guidance as you strive to reach your goals. So make it one of your goals to find a mentor or coach.

WORKBOOK

Chapter 6 Questions

Question: What mentors or coaches have you had in the past? How have you benefited from these relationships?

_____

_____

_____

_____

_____

_____

_____

_____

_____

_____

_____

Question: Who is your mentor now? How did you first connect with this person? Or alternatively, who might make a good mentor for your current point on your path to success—and why?

_____

_____

_____

_____

_____

_____

_____

_____

_____

_____

Question: What are you willing to put into your relationships with mentors or coaches?

_____

_____

_____

_____

_____

_____

_____

_____

_____

_____

_____

Action: Find a mentor who will invest in you, hold you accountable by calling it like it is, and encourage you to take specific steps forward on your path to success. Be willing to listen to your mentor or coach so their experience and expertise can provide you a significant boost toward your goals.

Chapter 6 Notes

CONCLUSION

Staying the Course

Everyone wants to be successful. I hear it every day: "I want to be successful."

Success is simple, but we can make it complicated. It isn't about extravagance—about mansions and sports cars and fancy-sounding job titles—but about bringing balance to the way we invest in relationships, our job, and ourselves on the road to accomplishing our goals.

Too many people try to complicate the term *success*. They think it means lots of money or material possessions—like a healthy bank account, nice clothes, or expensive jewelry.

But that's just not true.

How I define success is simple, and I invite you to share in this definition. Ready?

Setting and achieving goals is success. That's it. When you set and achieve goals for yourself, then you're successful.

Success Is Simple!

That said, people need to understand there are different levels and layers to success.

I met recently with my friend, Al Riddick, who is an entrepreneur and author of *The Uncommon Millionaire*.[8] During our discussion about goals and success, Al said, "Most people usually relate success with money. Success is nothing more than doing what you said you would do. As a perfect example, you said you would meet me at my office this morning at 8:30 a.m. You were on time. Therefore, you are a success. It's the daily behaviors we exhibit that produce our success—or lack thereof."

Once you reach a goal, there's always that next level, phase, or layer that exists, which we must tackle, and it looks different for each of us. The idea is to keep going and challenging yourself because success is not supposed to stop.

I'm not supposed to be successful today and unsuccessful tomorrow. Success is not a thing that just happens; success is a process of doing what we said we would do by setting and achieving goals on a continuing basis.

In short, success will be different for every one of us, but the important thing to remember is to keep challenging yourself.

You don't just graduate from high school and say, "That's it! I'm successful." No, you challenge yourself and say, "Where do I want to be five years from now, and how will I get there?" Or, "Where do I want to be in ten years, and how will I get there?"

How about you? Where do you want to be in five and ten years? What will you do to get there?

What's Next?

The most pertinent questions are "Where do I go from here?" and, above all, "How do I get there?"

If the goal is to get a job in a certain field, then you have to understand the market and competition to know how you will make it happen.

Some tools and resources can help you with this process, which is why we've already talked about planners, tools, mentors, and coaches. And then there's your environment—and the people whom you allow into that environment.

The people I'm associated with are not just average people who want to go to work and make money. The people I allow into my environment want to keep going. They are full of purpose and know life is about so much more than money. They understand that it's about fulfillment, love, caring, and family. They believe in outreach; they believe in making a difference.

When you're in a position to live stress-free and have lots of positive vibes and support, that's a part of success.

Because ultimately, success isn't just about you. For me, it's been about the people I've placed around me, the books I've read, and the relationships I've developed.

So set goals and achieve them to experience success. But don't forget along the way that success is about so much more than you.

Greatness Starts with Action

Massive action is a huge part of success; there must be a point when you step out and simply *do* it.

You don't think twice about it; you don't ponder about what could go wrong or about different hypothetical scenarios. You just need to go after it.

People will be surprised at the potential that lies within them. This goes back to my passion and purpose to motivate, inspire, and help individuals across all walks of life tap into their full potential through personal and professional development. I believe there is more in each of us. We all have the opportunity to tap into our inner greatness that we might not yet know exists!

Everyone has greatness within them. Everyone.

All of us have gone through different walks of life and experienced different paths. We all have different people surrounding us in our lives, and some of us have better access to certain things than others might.

But there's always opportunity. Nothing is ever hopeless.

It's easy to get caught up in the day-to-day grind and in comparing yourself to someone else. This creates confusion, frustration, and distraction. I encourage you to think differently and remember that true success is simple. Take full advantage of your opportunities to make your dreams, goals, and aspirations become reality.

With that said, what will *you* do?

You can either make it happen, or you can take a couple of steps back and wonder why it never happened. Which path is beckoning you?

Personal and professional development is all about investing in yourself. You are your biggest asset—so why *not* invest in yourself?

The ultimate difference between success and failure is persistence. One of my favorite success mottos, popularized by Zig Ziglar and others, is "It's not about where you start, it's about where you finish." As long as you do what you said you'd do and accomplish your goals, then you're successful.

Never forget that success is a process, however. It may take you one year, five years, or twenty years to reach your goal. Don't lose heart. Unlike milk, goals and dreams don't have expiration dates on them. Success is the outcome of staying on the course until you reach your destination.

And remember, the longer the climb, the more beautiful the view from the top.

With an active, persistent, balanced approach to life, success in every respect is yours for the taking.

Go after it. Take action and make it happen!"

Notes

1. Canaves, Sky. "Shanghai Building Nearly Collapses." *Wall Street Journal.* June 29, 2009. https://blogs.wsj.com/china-realtime/2009/06/29/shanghai-building-collapses-nearly-intact.
2. Mandela, Nelson. *Notes to the Future: Words of Wisdom.* Atria Books, 2012, p. 101.
3. Johnson, Tory and Robyn Freedman Spizman. *Women for Hire's Get-ahead Guide to Career Success.* Perigree Book, 2004.
4. Swindoll, Charles. *Improving Your Serve.* Word, 1981.
5. Sinek, Simon. "How Great Leaders Inspire Action." September 2009. *TED.* TED Conferences, LLC. https://www.ted.com/talks/simon_sinek_how_great_leaders_inspire_action.
6. Diamond, Dan. "Just 8% of People Achieve Their New Year's Resolutions. Here's How They Do It." *Forbes.* January 1, 2013. https://www.forbes.com/

sites/dandiamond/2013/01/01/just-8-of-people-achieve-their-new-years-resolutions-heres-how-they-did-it/#334f8f12596b.

7. The ESV® Bible (*The Holy Bible, English Standard Version®*). ESV® Text Edition: 2016. Crossway (a publishing ministry of Good News Publishers), 2001.

8. Riddick, Alfred D., Jr. *The Uncommon Millionaire: Financial Success Begins with Behavior.* Game Time Budgeting, 2016.

About the Author

Garrett Lee is the founder of Garrett Lee Speaks, LLC. Garrett is also an author, motivational speaker, education consultant, and active leader in his community. His purpose is to motivate, inspire, and help individuals and organizations tap into their full potential through personal and professional development. Garrett believes that everyone has the ability to tap into their inner greatness that they might not know exists!

Over the years, Garrett has spoken for a variety of clients, including high schools, colleges, universities, non-profit organizations, corporations, and the U.S. Air Force. As a result, many people have been strongly affected by his keynote presentations and workshops. Garrett's messages, presentations, and workshops have added tremendous value to the lives of his audience members.

Garrett has a huge passion for living, learning, and helping others achieve massive success. Over the years, he has invested lots of his time, energy, and money into his personal and professional development. One of Garrett's keys to success is investing in great mentors. Garrett has been very fortunate to have worked with some highly experienced coaches and mentors who are successful entrepreneurs.

About once a quarter, Garrett gives back to his community by volunteering to help with local non-profit organizations. While being fortunate to live a life that some may never get to experience, Garrett believes in paying forward and giving back while making an impact.

Feel free to reach out and connect with Garrett!

www.GarrettLeeSpeaks.com

Garrett@GarrettLeeSpeaks.com

Facebook and YouTube: @GarrettLeeSpeaks

LinkedIn: @Garrett Lee

About Speak It To Book

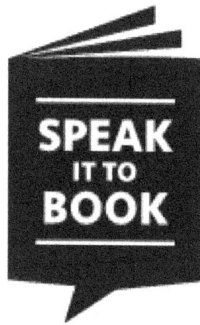

Speak It to Book is revolutionizing how books are created and used.

Traditional publishing requires thousands of hours, and then you're asked to surrender your rights. Self-publishing is indicative of a poor-quality product with no prestige. And neither model boasts results-driven marketing.

That's why we created a better option. Speak It To Book has the attention of the industry because we are disrupting it in a brilliant way.

Imagine:

- What if you had a way to get those ideas out of your head?
- What if you could get your story in front of the people who need it most?
- What if you took the next step into significance and influence?

You can accomplish all of these goals by writing a book. Plus, you can do it without having to use a pencil, and in less than one-tenth of the time!

Your ideas are meant for a wider audience. So step into significance—by speaking your story into a book.

Visit www.speakittobook.com to learn more.

www.ingramcontent.com/pod-product-compliance
Lightning Source LLC
Chambersburg PA
CBHW070055100426
42740CB00013B/2844